Ms. Understood

REMESSAGING THE JOURNEY FROM HEALING TO WHOLENESS

KIMBERLY R. TAYLOR

Enjoy the journey...
Esteem yourself!

Kimberly R. Taylor
2018

Ms. Understood
Remessaging the Journey from Healing to Wholeness
Kimberly R. Taylor

Copyright © 2014 Kimberly R. Taylor

Published by:
Kissed Publications
P. O. Box 9819
Hampton, VA 23670

ISBN-13: 978-0966760965
ISBN-10: 0966760964

For my parents,
Leon and Fannie Taylor.
Your love is everything to me.

.

Foreword

You always deal with my stuff. I like my stuff, it's mine. If you take it from me, what do I get in return?

In a compelling and sometimes humorous format, *Ms. Understood* dares to speak clearly and without fluff the fact that when God deals with "our stuff" it usually spells crisis for us. Crisis, a disruption of things as they were, is necessary and essential for emotional and spiritual growth to take place. Obvious crisis might be a child gone astray; an unexpected death of a loved one; a love that is lost; an unexpected medical diagnosis; losing a job; being cheated on; cheating on; breaking the law and getting caught; or breaking the law and not getting caught and living daily in fear; all represent opportunities to make new meanings out of life's experiences. Less obvious crisis are often signaled by a growing discomfort with the way things are, a paradigm shift, a spiritual epiphany that places you out of step with all of the people you have loved, and been loved by for years. Whenever the rules people have built their lives around begin to fail them, they enter into a crisis.

What happens when everything we think is supposed to happen does not occur in the manner or timing we expected? What happens when we choose to live by all the rules we were taught were important, only to discover that there are no real guarantees in life, and our only assurance is that what ever we are faced with, that grace will be sufficient? What happens when it feels as though you are in the middle of your very own tsunami? Growth happens, tremendous growth that could only be achieved through a breaking up process that allows for a reshaping of self.

Living a spiritual life is not new for Kimberly Taylor. The eldest daughter of a Pentecostal pastor and wife, she consistently tried to live a perfect and holy life, only to discover the human experience is wrought with unexpected twists and turns, mountain top experiences as well as deep foreboding valleys. Kimberly has weathered the worst of the storm and has with unique insight and humor retraced her journey to greater spiritual depth. Previously embraced scriptural nuggets and everyday cliché's: "behind every dark cloud there is a silver lining", and with "God all things are possible" become barely audible and sometimes downright irritating when you are seeking comfort from another human being when in the midst of a crisis. Sometimes you just want someone to say, "You are right, that is real messed up". Thanks to Kimberly Taylor, *Ms. Understood* does just that.

Dr. Barbara Quinney Tobias
Clinical Psychologist
Visionary and Director of the Relationship Academy

ACKNOWLEDGMENTS

I acknowledge the following wonderful persons with my sincerest gratitude:

I thank God. In a world where God's existence is questioned, I honor God as the center, the source, resource, and joy of my life. While clearly I do not understand everything about You, everything I do know is wonderful. I am truly humbled that you love me flaws and all.

Thanks to my editor and publisher, Kimberly T. Matthews and Kissed Publications, for guiding me through this new and wonderful landscape of authorship.

My parents, Pastor Leon and Mrs. Fannie Taylor who did not always know what God was up to with me, but knew God was doing something, and knowing that at some point it would be all right. Thanks for loving me through everything.

My siblings, Kyra, Keisha, and Kevin, you are the witnesses to my whole life, I could not have picked better people to go through my life with. Thank you for having my nieces and nephews. Auntie Kim loves them all: Jonathan, Kevin, Ezekiel, Christian, Zekiera, Gianna and not to be outdone or overlooked, Cowgirl Rockstar Princess Jordan.

To Ricky, thank you for everything from the very beginning.

To all of my aunts, uncles, cousins, cousins- cousins, cousins-kids and anybody else who believes and could quite possibly be my relative, ain't nobody quite like family. We may not have it all together, but together we have it all.

Dr. D. Maurice Green, before there were others, there was you. Thanks for a lifetime of friendship both in and out of our various transitions. Onward to self- actualization!

Thecla Brown Avery Cotton, Jamie Crawford, Janene Jackson, Markci Metcalf, Brian Perkins, and Jackie Thompson: these are the people who saw me at my most vulnerable and still championed me.

Linda Lonzer, thanks for providing shelter in the time of my storm.

Love and hugs to my extraordinarily talented and gifted God-children, Mikalah and Justin.

I am entirely indebted to two spectacular, spiritual midwives Dr. Barbara Q. Tobias and Nurse Practitioner Theresa Richardson, without your superb midwifery the story of my life would be vastly different. You have labored with me through the most trying time of my own metamorphosis. I have been enriched greatly by your skill and strength. Thanks for holding my hands, while I relearned to walk.

I have been forever changed by these Daughters of Thunder who personally have made indelible imprints in my spiritual journey, Rev. Dr. Carolyn L. Gordon, Rev. Dr. Jacqueline Thompson, Rev. Dr. Susie C. Owens, Rev. Dr. Delores Carpenter, Rev. Dr. Cheryl J. Sanders, Rev. Dr. Kelly Brown Douglas, Rev. Dr. Paulette L. Scott, Rev. Dr. Karen Mc Nair, Co- Pastor Gloria Adams and Rev. Jacqueline Waldo. Thank you is not even sufficient.

To anyone who has this book, every sleepless night, prayer in agony, every deferred dream, every minute of wandering and wondering has led to the text that you have, the path was not easy but it is worth it. I encourage you to share your journey with others, so that fewer of us feel alone.

Take a chance on yourself and your dreams,

Kimberly R. Taylor

TABLE OF CONTENTS

1. The Journey Begins 1

2. Wanderings and Musings 13

3. Remessaging Wanderings and Musing 27

4. Self-Care 29

5. Remessaging Self-Care 39

6. Destiny 43

7. Remessaging Destiny 53

8. Conversation 57

9. Remessaging Conversation 69

1. The Journey Begins

You have this book in your hand, because I needed this book in my hand. I looked for a book that could be a soundtrack and a guide against the crazy experiences in my life. After looking for about two years, I did not find the right book. I'd read great books, but not ones that fully convinced me to rejoin life fully and completely. Nothing convinced me to be present as a leading voice, instead of the background player role I had perfected. In my search, I got the emotional equivalent of a plink; it was like hitting a really bad chord on an acoustic guitar. Plink. Plink. Pop. I wanted my heart to sing again, but the tunes were off. There was no coach, no cheerleader, and no choral director who could assuage me or who could teach me words to a song I'd not sung before. Confidence. Security. Boldness. Pizzazz. Adventurous. Contentment. Peaceful. Easy. It's crazy knowing you and your life is supposed to sing and be a song, and to open yourself, your voice to this thing called life and have complete laryngitis. I desperately wanted to chime into the happiness around me, but I could not, I lost my voice. How do you learn to speak and sing again? Simply change the conversation. This book is a journey into the conversation we need to have with ourselves when our hearts are broken, our lives seem shattered and tomorrow seems likes forever. There is a somewhere over the rainbow. There is a song that follows you and that follows after you.

Any cataclysmic event that shakes you and asks the question what are you doing with yourself now will qualify you to understand this text. That event for me was depression. For some it may be childbirth, graduation, marriage, divorce, chronic sickness, job loss, death, a family feud, or separation of any kind. You are now in a defining moment, brought about in a crisis and orchestrated by God. There is no right or wrong way to handle what you facing. You probably have heard many opinions about how to deal with your particular scenario. This book assumes that you need to be reminded of what you know innately. It is encouragement. Because encouragement and a gentle nudge sometimes is all that we can handle, until we can convince ourselves to move a little further.

I now view life as a journey. Along the path, some of the terrain is smooth, some bumpy, and some completely turbulent. Major Depression with an Anxiety Disorder was my completely turbulent moment. Calling my girlfriend and having a good cry was not the remedy. I was having a near major meltdown. I was fittin' ta go plumb crazy, or so I thought. Trust me, it wasn't even cute. And to make matters worse, apparently, I had been that way before. I just didn't know it. Over the years, I had tricked myself into believing that it was something else. I didn't know that's what it was. I was so good at fooling myself all those other times. And I did it for years and called it many other things. Somehow I was able to fool myself into thinking that I was ok.

Previously, I'd always managed to get over 'it'. The 'it' being those smaller episodes of depression. I generally got over it by overspending, overeating or over indulging in a relationship that was not in my best interest. At the height, or depth of my depression (whichever term is best) it was no longer repressed, but began to ooze out of me like the disgusting yellow, indeterminable filling of a pimple on the face of a teen invaded by the ravages of acne. I had reached a point where I couldn't keep it together. I was just a mess, crying all the time and shutting down in pieces. My confidence was shaken; my spirit was shattered; and my soul was completely numb. Depression was a juncture; both a crisis, and a growth enabler.

I knew that God was out of God's mind for even having me go through this depression stuff. I was a very unwilling participant. Isn't it something how God does not consult us on what tests and trials we go through? God just gives us grace to go through. In my circle of friends I was the advice giver, the consoler, the wise one. I was the "mother." But this time, I needed help. I did not want to feel anything. There had to be a solution to the pain. I wanted a numbness to overwhelm the numbness I was already feeling. I was so desperate to erase my pain. Nothing mattered more than getting out of my emotional black hole. Depression is a very lonely place; the emptiness is a dense vortex, where nothing seems close enough to remedy the problem. I considered every option known. I couldn't afford the financial excess of crack or alcohol, nor did I have the time to spare for the devastating physical effects of illegal substances. No man was available to distract me. Suicide may have been a solution, except I could not figure out a way to do it without pain. I believed that my friends were growing tired of my tirades. I started shutting down, and shutting them out. But I had to do something to numb the pain, at least. So I got a therapist. I wasn't sure if I was going crazy; but it felt like it. I got the therapist because at least I had health insurance, and I could afford the $15 co-pays. At the time, I thought I was going to therapy to help me get things back to normal. I was just trying to get my mojo back, so that I could return to the grind that had become my life.

Initially, one of the reasons why I went to therapy is because I had several unexplainable illnesses, which did not chart on MRI's, EKG's and other physical exams I was taking every three weeks to try to figure out why my body was rebelling against me. So I figured maybe something was wrong with my head. And then there was that uncontrollable crying. By the way, numbness, undiagnosable illness, and relentless crying are very clear signs of clinical depression. In those early days of therapy, I cried before the session, during the session and after the session. I was so sick of crying. I was already doing that before I went there, and here she was making me cry some more. I appreciated my therapist for listening. However, I absolutely did not appreciate the work she required. I wanted to quit so many times, but instinctually I knew, my gut was telling me, there was more to me going through than just going through. Something was happening; I just couldn't put my hands on it. So much introspection and investigation into myself was draining; and it was brutal, ugly work. Who knew that you could just get sick of talking about yourself? I did. But change was coming.

I believe in Divine Providence, and our relationship was too divinely ordered to ignore it. She reiterated that I had to go all the way through this experience for the benefit of the rest of my life, and for the lives that I was to impact. She spoke both medically and spiritually. At the time, I hung onto to those words from her, because I did not have the strength to create an alternate reality for myself. She saw this crisis as a catharsis, and the beginning and birthing of a new level of spirituality for me. Birth is never easy, natural or spiritual. She also likened my process at that time to an emotional constipation. She observed that I was so backed up (emotionally) that she had to pull some stuff out of me in chunks so that I could get a regular flow. Gross right? Yeah I know, imagine me hearing it for the first time. And imagine that I have never really gotten the image out of my head. I wanted so desperately to stop therapy then, but for a myriad of reasons at the time I had to continue, against my will. Eventually, my reasons for continuing with therapy became purer and personal. Thankfully, my therapist was as committed to me healing as I was faithful for attending, for whatever reasons compelled me to stay.

It seemed that too much was happening at once. I really believed that my head would explode from all the changes that were happening to me. I was in the midst of growing up.

An authentic growth will have you feeling like that. If you are experiencing a growth adjustment, just steady yourself, and sit with it. Get emotional. Don't get emotional. Pray. Don't pray. Question God; fuss at yourself. Whatever it feels like for you let it go. These kinds of changes that are emerging require you to pay attention to yourself and where you are headed on your journey. Whatever your defining moment is, you must clearly decide if you will change and grow or if you will allow the opportunity to overtake you.

Growing is a difficult and wonderful process. Into everyone's life there are some singular, defining, refining experiences. It happens many times during our lifetime. In retrospect, most of us can say that without those experiences; you would definitely be another person. More often than not those times of definition are fraught with pain and a whole lot of learning. Stagnation is a curse. If you are not growing, you are not going. And if you are not growing, what is the point? You are not going to become anything more than who or what you are right now, and that would be a pity. God requires more. Everything God made has a growth component, even us. I believe that God delights in seeing us evolve, change, transform and transcend even the notions of ourselves. Most of the learning we do in life is about ourselves. Ultimately, we learn what we can endure, validate what we know to be absolutely true, and what is most important in our lives and about ourselves. Real growth promotes real change. Life offers these opportunities for change and growth.

Unfortunately, everyone does not choose to grow, nor do they embrace the process. Here is what I now know for sure, it is best at least to expect change, even if you don't agree with it. I did not expect it. I did not want it, or so I thought. Change is frightening, unnerving and inevitable.

This text assumes that you are at a place where you probably don't hear God's voice or see God's hand; but you are aware that God simply is. I believe, the longer we are on the journey, we see God less. God is not less available, just not as visible as before. God cannot afford to be revealed to us the same ways as when we first encountered God. We would never learn to trust God fully. Our expectation would become that God would not change, and that every problem has the same solution. A parent's visual demands from a child will transition as a child ages. A teenager does not require the same attention from a parent that a preschooler or toddler does. The older a child gets, the child understands a parent's availability, skill, or love is not predicated upon a line of vision. However, a line of communication, an understanding and awareness that the parent is available has more impact than a sighting. Thus a child learns to call, if and when a parent is needed. Likewise, God understands, we would not grow, gain trust or have our faith expanded if God only showed Godself one way. It is because of the journey, that we know more about God. Isn't it better to know God, than it is to see God? If you really know God, then you know at some point you will see God, because God just does show up.

Life can dish out a doozie!   No, no, no, not the cute stuff that can be resolved in a couple of days, and you forget about it. A doozie is something you've got to go through. It changes you. Some people call these experiences a storm, a wilderness, a trial or tribulation. No matter what you call it, it is a part of life. Some crises are God ordered, while others are self-inflicted. Whatever their origins, critical moments in life can either break you or build you. Ultimately, you will learn something about you. It is during these moments where your character is revealed. In an extended crisis, some other stuff about you shows up too. You may discover some not so nice things about you, as well as areas of deficit. Then there comes a critical decision, do you keep the nasty stuff, or do you shed it and allow your character to be forged? Will you choose to emerge? Should you choose to fortify your character then I promise you that you are in for the long haul. You will have entered the growth process. Growth is a choice. Growth is not easy, but it is necessary. Growth is not a straight shot, all pretty and clean and without incident. If growth is a war, you are the casualty. Old notions, thoughts, and ways have to die.

Women are blessed to be able to handle multiple tasks, roles and identities. But for some of us, we lose us, while performing our duties. We can become so role- oriented that who God wants us to be disappears. This happened to me. I had allowed what I did, to define who I was. What I do, is not who I am! During my crisis, I discovered that what I learned previously, did work. It did for then. In retrospect, I believe that a crisis is really God's way for us to get on track with who we are to become beyond our roles. Did you ever notice, in a crisis that all of the "important stuff" is suspended, and we begin to do the work on ourselves that we often neglect? Because of our ability to handle multiples roles, as women, one of our greatest struggles is being all things for all people and remaining true to ourselves. To thine own self be true. That should be the 11th commandment. Listen up ladies, being all things to all people, ain't even possible. So if anybody in this world is going to be pleased with me, it might as well be me. And as long as I am not violating laws natural, spiritual and personal, let everybody else deal with the aftermath of that decision. Living in freedom of thought, mind, expression and spirit is absolutely priceless. I suspect that living like this is how God intends for us to enjoy our time on earth.

Embracing growth also involves accepting all the wonderful new shades of you. I was emerging and changing, somehow I missed it and did not know it. My crisis revealed my growth. Very often we can forget that we've grown past some points. We may even minimize our worth because of the crisis. Sometimes some life events last so long, or are so traumatizing that we begin to identify ourselves with the event rather than taking on the magnificent changes that come to light as a result. I was no longer a follower, but a leader, no longer a student but a teacher, no longer the novice, but the experienced. The tools that worked then, were failing me, yet I was still trying to construct my new world with tools that had the efficacy of a Fisher Price tool set. All truths are not transferable. That is to say, some stuff that worked for me, no longer did. It was time to get a new language. But Lord knows how I tried, and tried and tried not to change. There was nothing wrong with the old stuff; it just was not going to work in a new place.

It can seem that every now and then we lose our way. But in losing we gain so much. Our paths are ordered. So even being "lost" is a part of the plan. As you journey and transform, it is important to remember that there is no right or wrong way. There is only the way that God has chartered for you.

Very often during this laborious process, I had to literally encourage myself. I had to discover my new voice. A new crisis erases old landmarks. I had no markers for this unearthed part of myself. My therapist suggested that I write in a journal. Writing would contrast what I was saying to myself. I had gone through so much; my thinking had gone askew. She called it cognitive restructuring. She explained that there was direct connection between what you internalize, or say to yourself, and how you feel. Writing would be the tool of restating. It was almost like remessaging myself. (Did I just invent a word?) Of course, I didn't always do it. That would be too much like right. Eventually, I was forced into writing because I was so emotionally blocked up that I literally could emote all day. I had a lot of words in me. Some of it negative, some of it positive, most of it seemingly confusing. All of it was how I felt on my journey. So to rid myself of so many thoughts, I would have to move in with her for 24- hour psychotherapy, or either add a splendid new white jacket with no sleeves and many buckles to my wardrobe for everyday wear. Neither was an attractive option, for her (the former) or me (the latter); so I wrote.

During this crisis, I had to say the words, the meanings, the metaphors and the emotions that would propel me forward. This book contains the words and images I had to tell myself to get through these new experiences. I had to begin to believe some of this stuff; or I would have seriously lost it. Sage wisdom instructs us that as long as you are going through, you ain't stuck. I did not want to be stuck anymore. I didn't believe any of what I am saying now on the outer level of me. But the inner me knew that what I was saying had a truth. I share this truth with you. I know it is not for everybody. But it is for somebody, because I don't believe we have experiences only for them to languish in isolation. I am richer, for even sharing them on paper.

As I said before, growth is not a straight shot, or a straight path. Growth hurts; but in the end it is good. Look back over some of the crisis you've already overcome. Can't you say that you are better for having gone through it? You would be a different person had you not. Please also remember rarely are our experiences for ourselves. Our lives are designed to be a witness for someone you have yet to encounter. The lessons and strength that carries you through ultimately become strength for someone else.

I do not have an auspicious reason as to why this text was written. Simply, I never developed the discipline for journaling. I still don't have it. But when I was going through, I wished, oh I wished there was a book that had something I could reference to get me out of my quagmire. But alas, no such book existed for me. So I started writing something I could read to give me a little kick in the pants. I would read it and reflect until I got to the next place. This is the book I needed. There are many books on the market that inspire. Many are in my library, but where they failed me during this time was that they were too lengthy. As a scholar, I felt obligated to engage the whole book. What I needed was a jolt! I didn't have the time or the strength to digest a great big old book. After all, I was completely involved with being depressed. But I could manage to read something for about a month. It couldn't be too deep, but it had to be compelling. And I would reflect on that information, sort of like chewing on a mental cud until I could gather enough strength for the next part of the journey. I wrote what I needed. I offer that same style here. Read it all at once, as daily inspiration, or as needed.

As I began writing, I found that I could not really write directly to myself. So I began a conversation with myself. I spoke to the part of me that needed to comprehend what my life was and where it was going. I spoke to myself in the third person and to absorb the shock of this new language that was developing in me. So Dear Journal became Ms. Understood. Why, Ms. Understood? For years I operated on principles and theories that I understood to be ok for me at a particular time in my life. Age, circumstance, maturity, role changes had all converged and displaced my prior beliefs about myself. Inevitably, I felt like I missed what I understood. So in order to re- train myself I had to understand myself not as a little girl, but as a woman; as a Ms. who now understands? Understand?

Remessage is not in any dictionary I own. A web search usually took my entry as *Re: Message*. Technically, remessage is not a word. It is the combining of a prefix and a noun. Remessaging the Journey is the phrase that I am using to tie up what is the balance of this book. Remessaging is the word that came to me when I was trying to analyze and summarize this new place in my life. I'll start with this definition to help you better appreciate the experiences and thoughts captured. Please look at some very basic definitions of the two core parts of the word remessage, which are the prefix re and the base word message.

Re is a prefix and is defined as: *with reference to; in connection with; concerning; again; anew.* Message is a noun and is defined as: *communication, or meaning* based on the Random House Unabridged Dictionary, © Random House, Inc. 2006.

The core parts of these definitions have been combined for our use.

Remessaging is defined as: Actions, thoughts and language with reference to and in connection with a new communication and meaning appropriate to our life journey, spoken to ourselves and lived in our lives.

As this book was being formed, I noticed that I was speaking several messages to the same areas of struggle. I divided those areas of struggle into subjects within this book: Wanderings and Musings, Self-Care, Destiny and Conversation. I was trying to re-tell, re-order, and redefine what I believed about myself and my internal talk. Unwittingly, I was remessaging my experience. Some things that meant one thing at another portion of my journey now had another insight. There seemed to be a Grand Canyon sized gulf of awareness between my younger and my now self. I had gained

> *Remessaging: actions, thoughts and language with reference to and in connection with a new communication and meaning appropriate to our life journey, spoken to ourselves and lived in our lives.*

some lessons. But with age and experience those lessons were being tested and challenged. Basically, I was wondering, did it mean what it meant? And in some cases, some thoughts just did not.

Remessaging as a term is similar to other formalized schools of thought. In my childhood, I learned a biblical scripture that said, as a man or woman thinks, so is (s)he. Life strategist, Rhonda Byrne calls it "The Secret", which is properly termed the Law of Attraction. Psychologists may call it Cognitive Behavioral Therapy. And now, I am adding this new word and thought, remessaging to this line of thinking. What each of these views has in common is the thought that you must somehow name and shape how you view your life journey. None of these thoughts suggest that life would be easier or missing its challenges. But they all converge on a singular thought, that our thoughts order our world, in whatever state we find ourselves.

However, what I have discovered in living is that even though you are living and while your life is transitioning you, it is also imperative that your language must also change along with the transition.

A conflict will ultimately emerge if the two do not ever get into alignment. Transitions yield transformations. Transitions offer new visions and new awareness. The most metamorphic transitions in our life can change our locations so radically that our language fails to catch up with where we have moved. So it is in that space, where we struggle. The struggle is between the old language and the new location

Finally, I am not my previous depression. Sometimes I still struggle, but that initial episode was just that. It was just a brief interruption before this next wonderful phase in my life. After all, you have this book in your hand, and in my old world, this most likely would have gotten written at age 60 and not 35. The experience was necessary for me to change my life, and to let go of some false notions about what makes a successful life. I am a confident, healing woman, who embraces the fact that change is inevitable, and that everything (that's right everything) works together for my good. And if it feels bad right now, no matter - that just means it ain't good yet. This text is birthed from my heart. That soft, squishy, malleable, hard as nails ticker that has been crushed, broken, repaired and crazy glued by my last count at least a kablillion, bazillion times. Get the crazy glue and tape out because you got next.

Please read this book as an inspirational guide, as motivation, as fuel. This journey presented here is part narrative, part lyrical, part rhetorical, part questioning, and part healing all combining to facilitate wholeness. You can digest it all at once, or like medicine as needed. To maximize the new places you are headed for in your heart, at the end of each section are guided questions for your consideration that will help you practice remessaging your own new wonder- filled journey.

Enjoy the journey.

2. WANDERINGS AND MUSINGS

Intro to Wanderings and Musings

Remessaging a wandering mode is tricky. It can look like indecision, playing around or being clueless. Sometimes no direction is direction. Our unconscious is trying to lead us to our destiny. Random thoughts provide significant clues into how we should live our lives authentically. The majority of us don't live in our destiny, and that same majority tends to tune out our unconscious leanings. Fortunately, God through our unconsciousness supplies us with reminders throughout our lives, of our greatest selves. Certain thoughts, desires, dreams and hopes never die. Try as we might to distract ourselves with less than providential pursuits. Wanderings and musings give us initial clues to our greatness and our God despite what life looks like right now.

&

Dear God:

I wish you would consult with me a little more often about these trials and tribulations you conjure up for me. I could give you some advice about me, if you would just ask.

Here's my opinion on the whole thing about making changes in me and all. Often they are inconvenient, last too long and reveal stuff about me that I do not care to be reminded of.

Sometimes I wish we could just compromise. You know just come to the table before you try and change me… AGAIN. I am just really getting used to the new me from the last situation, and here we go again, with more changes.

Some days I like the fact that I am a negative, procrastinating, angry, and fearful. It is who I am. Ok, I don't necessarily like it either, but at least I am comfortable with it. The changes you've got planned for me, well that's not so comfortable or convenient.

You always deal with my stuff. I like my stuff. It's mine. If you take it from me what do I get in return?

Oh yeah, I do become more like you and less like me. With all of these trials and changes, sometimes I forget.

P. S. Since I have got to go through, can you at least let it be 72 degrees with no rain? And can I have good movies on cable, when I am ready to watch them… is that too much to ask?

P.P. S. I need ice cream.

Fear

Scared to live.

Scared to die.

Scared to cry.

Scared to feel.

Scared to move forward.

Scared to move backward.

Scared to believe dreams can come true.

Scared to believe that I make a difference.

Scared to try new things.

Scared of old things.

My body is paralyzed,

I feel blood running in my veins,

Which is a clear signal that I have not met my Maker.

But it's a blood that runs cold at the thought of trying again.

I fell and I hurt myself.

I saw my own blood, and it scared me.

I tasted my own tears.

I've cried enough to fill a tub.

I've cried for the old and I've cried for the new.

Today I am paralyzed with fear.

Where do you go when there is no map for the journey?

There are no voices to guide.

There are no hands to hold.

There are no trails to follow.

I know that I am not the first, and won't be the last.

But I feel like the first and the only.

Only meaning LONELY.

Scared to try.

Scared I am missing something.

Scared to mess up.

Scared to be.

Scared to emerge.

Scared out of my mind, scared in my body, scared in my soul.

Time has tempered me and made me conscious of pain, aware of roadblocks, aware of delay and denial. As I sit paralyzed, in the quietness, acknowledging the fear, there is a voice that I remember that is faint. Not quite mute, barely audible, nevertheless, there.

It is there? Is it there? What is it? Something of the old me and the emerging me wonders what it is, buried underneath the rumble and wreckage, which are my many emotions. It is gasping for air, waiting for me to dig it up, to discover it, rediscover it, to uncover it, to dust it off, clean it off, and use it again, use it daily, use it, share it, incorporate it into the fabric of my soul. It is faith. It is hope.

Fear had no voice that I recognized, it talked but I ignored it for a long time. On occasion I heard it, but I did not care. My youth did not befriend it. But with age, I invited it in. I did not ask it to become prominent in my life; it is now an unwelcome guest in my home, having ordered me around. Fear is an unwelcome housemate, refusing to go. Letting me know that I have no other friends but it.

"No one will stay with you, while you are like this. No one is there for you all day every day, all night every night like me. Happiness comes and goes, Peace stays awhile, contentment; it is a joke. But I am here. And above all where is your God?" It taunts.

Fear says, "Any power I have, you gave me. But I don't surrender such tools as easily as you did. I am aware that I have stayed awhile. But I will not go easily, if at all. You have fed, nurtured, and clothed me. I am healthy and strong. I am here. Every day you sat with me, talked with me, your doubt and negativity fed and strengthened me."

But I say, "Fear has worn out its welcome. I want you to go, so that I can get my life back. I want my life back."

I want to breathe and appreciate it. I want to see clearly, and appreciate what I see. I want to hear and like what I am hearing. I want to believe what people believe about me. I want to see what they see about me. I want to hear what they hear about me. I want to speak the same language that everyone else speaks about me. But fear has become a translator for me, I say or do nothing without conferring with it. Fear is not a wise counsel. Fear is a poor companion. Fear is not a friend, but an enemy who disguises itself as comfort, as solitude as safety. I would like for you to find a new residence. But I fear that you will not leave without a fight- a real fight that I fear I am not ready for YET.

A Day at the Nail Shop

By my own admission, I previously was not a good relaxer, as in one who relaxes. I wouldn't call myself a workaholic. But when I was not working, I was just a person who was very, very unclever during her free time. My down time was spent sleeping, eating, or getting ready for the next big thing. In the early days of my depression, I was given the assignment to try new things, social situations and activities that were calming. I can't tell you how hard it was for me to "learn" not to work so hard and to let go and enjoy the moments. The following is one of my lessons in relaxing.

I had to learn how to relax. I was being forced to relax. Just RELAX! This was the hardest thing I ever, ever had to do. Of all the things I had accomplished with my life, at the age of 33, I had managed to never darken the doors of a nail salon. Sure I'd heard about the pedi-mani, but who had time for that. It was something that I'd never shared with too many, and when I did they found it completely incredulous, that I did not relish in such indulgences. But these days, I had nothing but time. Time to work on relaxation. Time to work on therapy. Time for new discoveries about my old self. One such discovery was this much neglected area of self –care.

My body was screaming if you do not learn how to do this; I will shut down, until I am ready to move. For once I listened, reluctantly; even regrettably I sought out the nearest nail shop. Before now, there was no need to spend real money on something as frivolous as spending money on myself. I was too frightened.

I took the bravest person I knew with me, Mikalah, my seven-year - old goddaughter. For days she had been screaming how she wanted to look good in her new sandals. She refused to even wear them because none of her cousins could properly polish her toenails.

When we arrived, the nail shop was packed. Women were spilling secrets. Men were overseeing the fine- tuning and tweaking of their women's appendages, rummaging through their pockets for enough $20's to pay for the full mani-pedi treatment. Even some women were engaging in the same pocket hunt for their women. It seemed like everyone knew something that I did not know. The smell of acrylic and lotions and potions nearly overwhelmed me. This was not the familiar smell of printer ink, copier toner or blue pens that previously ordered my days. People were smiling and chitchatting at each other. This was definitely unlike the office atmosphere where things got so rushed and crazy that the sublimely ridiculousness of office politics became normalcy.

Mikalah skipped into the shop, very happily behind me. I on the other hand felt like I was walking the final mile before the death row chamber. How dare someone tell me to learn to relax? And how is the nail shop the panacea?

Mikalah looked at the wall of nail polish. She moved her hands up and down the wall, as if she were perusing a box of Crayola. She could barely contain herself. She sat in the closest chair, hoping this would accelerate her being escorted to the foot tub. I had such a sense of dread. Mikalah picked up on my apprehension and asked me a question.

"Don't you like to get your feet done?" I told her that it was my first time. Unfazed, she replied, "You will like it. I love getting my feet done."

She held my hand for about 30 seconds. Because of the anxiety built up in my body, I began to shake. Without saying a word, she sat in my lap, and we played hand games, Ms. Mary Mack and Slide.

Eventually, we were led back to the foot chambers. An Asian lady, named Wendy was my torturer. She smiled.

"They always smile before they kill you." I thought.

She led me back to the row of foot bowls attached to chairs.

"How odd?" I thought.

She asked, "Jus you? "

"No," I said. "Her too."

"Oh, how sweet; I get her next."

As the water began to fill the basin and the foot powders turned the water blue, Mikalah's smile began to grow with extreme delight. My feet were submerged in the soapy abyss. I imagined that I was anywhere else but there. Mikalah's words brought me back from my outer body experience.

"Doesn't it feel good? Don't you like it? I know that you will like it, I can't wait to get mine done."

As wonderful as Mikalah is her questions impaled me, not because she asked, but because of my uncertainty of how to navigate through this exercise in relaxation. She was my audience of one, and I never wanted her to believe that I did not know something. In most areas of my life, I had answers, but I felt like a dunce, at this the simplest of tasks.

I chose red, not because I knew that's what I wanted, but because it is the color of people of courage or so I thought. When the whole ordeal was done, I began to get many compliments on my toes.

I liked it three days later.

Questions with No Answers

"Now what?"

"What next?"

"Do you know what you are doing?"

"Are you sure?"

These questions plague me. They follow me wherever I go. I try to recall how I made it through before. And I did make it before. Try as I may to recall the details of past adventures, I am fuzzy on the details. It seems too long ago. It seems childish to me, almost like a game. I remember that it hurt then too, but not like this. Nothing has hurt like this before.

With these queries, I am being haunted by my past, harassed by my present, and taunted by the future. I have no answer. I have no guess, no hypothesis good enough to begin to address the questions.

The questions hound me. "You should be able to answer one of us. It's not that difficult. If you can answer just one of us, then you can get on with life again. You do remember how you sailed through your days, without a real thought don't you? Life was automatic. Remember that?"

I do remember. I remember security. I remember predictability. I remember sameness. I was raised to want it. Taught to love it. Baptized in its religiosity.

But that cost me something too. I gave up my essence for conformity, originality for protocol. I lost my uniqueness and myself and embraced someone else's vision of a comfortable existence for me. Individuality, innovation, inspiration were placed on the auction block and as a result, my soul was shackled and bound, with my soul's emancipation, only a dream.

I forgot to breathe. God breathed into me the breath of life. He breathed himself into me. I forgot to exhale. I began to suffocate under the carbon dioxide of purposelessness. Faintly, I challenge the questions.

Why can't I?

Who says I am not able?

Remembering my place and licking my wounds from the recent confrontation, I back down from the challenge, not realizing whose voice is speaking through me now. I don't know where it came from. Fear returns me to normalcy.

The tone of the voices within is split. It is defiant to the challenge and resistant to the change. Each emotion has equal amounts of my trust and confidence. I come back to my senses and shut my mouth.

Another battle in the war for my soul's purpose and sanity is engaged. I am not strong enough to continue. Where I am weak the Spirit gives utterance. It speaks, "You can. You will. You already are."

As the Spirit speaks, my humanity minimizes and diminishes what my heart knows for sure. With lackluster faith, my filtered response becomes "Maybe. Maybe not."

"Yeah, that's what we thought," the questions taunt and jeer in a symphonic chorus. "Many people dare not challenge us. Many people don't. Most won't. Count yourself among the many, who do not overcome so easily. If you could answer us, then you gain access to another realm." Consider yourself among the ordinary."

I wonder in my soul, if destiny prevails over doubt, especially when doubt is heavier and destiny is distant. But because the Spirit spoke, new questions engage me and pick up the fight where my courage waned. They ask:

"How high?"

"How long?"

"How much?"

"Is the pain worth it?"

"Is the journey greater than the destination?"

"Can you endure yourself if you don't?"

"Will you journey again?"

I can only answer one of these questions. I have no answers for the others today.   I pray, "Only if you help me again. I will. I will. I will. I think."

Ok with Being Ok

- Is it ok that I don't like the gym?

- Is it ok that I don't want to be with him?

- Is it ok, that I hate my job, and desire to create my own destiny, full and free.

- Is it ok, that I cry by myself, and then laugh with you?

- Is it ok that I'm not yet ready to move?

- Why should I do more than I already do?

- I have not yet learned to thrive where I am, before I have been told that now that I have to move.

- Sure I will, and you know that I will, but can I just enjoy the scenery here, before I make the next turn?

- In this moment, at this time I am still.

- Is it ok to lounge around in my pajamas, and not answer the phone?

- While I love my friends, I also love being alone.

- Is it ok to listen to Wynonna Judd and Bonnie Raitt?

- Boogie down with Fantasia, Raheem Divine and Anthony Hamilton as we lay.

- Is it ok to be a freak, a hoochie, a scholar and a lady?

- I am not just all or nothing, I am both and.

- Is it ok to watch the old Super friends and then flip to CNN?

- Is it ok to be traditional at home and independent out there?

- Is it ok, that I want whom I want when I want, and believe that I don't have to settle?

- Is it ok that I don't fit the mold?

- Some days, I am selfish by design, other times I may give totally, nearly depleting.

- Is it ok to merge my corporate self with my supportive self?

- Anything less than all this will diminish me.

- But if I learn to be ok with being ok, maybe then I can flourish.
- Can I ascend and descend like a Phoenix,
- Having legendary strength while waiting?
- Is it ok to rhyme some lines because I understand time? Or break the meter, the written structure while other times I allow my thoughts to ramble.
- Is it ok that I change my mind in the middle of a sentence?
- Can I retract what I did, when I know that's not best for me?
- Can I just be me without apology?

Ok for me is all of these things that I know about me, and many more things that I don't know about me. I just want to be ok with being ok.

Ms. Understood: Taking Inventory

Life is measured in the things that are most valuable to you, whether or not others understand them is immaterial. Here's what matters most today:

- 1300 in the bank
- 1100 due in bills
- 1 robe for preaching
- 6 black suits
- 3 clerical collars
- 2 TVs with remotes
- 15 Tyler Perry DVD's (no bootlegs)
- 1 radio with a cassette, because I still like my tapes
- 100's of childhood memories
- 1,000's of dreams yet to be fulfilled
- 1 box of Crunch 'n Munch
- 1 pair of drumsticks, just in case the urge returns
- 2 computers
- 3 jump drives
- 730 days out of work
- 3 novels in the making
- 98,000 in student loans
- 2 earned degrees
- 200 sessions of therapy
- 20mg of Prozac
- 300 songs written, many more forgotten
- 2 parents in their 60s married and still in love
- 3 siblings who are the witnesses to my life
- 7 nieces and nephews who think I am the greatest and know the most

- 1 dozen crabs
- 536 songs captured on my I-phone
- 7 sets of sheets
- 4 comforters
- 65 pairs of drawers, enough so that I don't have to wash until I feel like it
- 7 boxes of cereal on my shelf, 3 healthy and 4 of the stuff I loved as a kid
- 1 best boyfriend and 1 best girlfriend
- 4 road dawgs, who see me through everything
- 3 gray hairs Mikalah always find when combing my hair
- 30 trips to Disney World
- 3 serious relationships
- 3 bad breakups
- 1 loving broken and mended heart
- 5 fingers that are held and protected by five that are not my own
- 8 years my junior
- 9 months of dating
- 8 months of happiness
- 7 months of knowing that I am truly in love

This is the inventory of my life, 0 regrets

A Perfect Day

There is gloomy weather outside. But it is warm inside, because I did pay electricity bill. My red T –shirt matches my Mickey Mouse pajama bottoms. My hair is tied down. The couch is my home. The black comforter is my protector.

- The Color Purple. Check.
- Tyler Perry's DVD collection. Check.
- My momma's okay. Check.
- My daddy's okay. Check.
- My sibling's ok. Check.
- Ringer Turned off. Check.
- Popcorn. Check.
- Banana popsicles are in the fridge, ½ of one is in my hand.
- Look across the room, there is a pile of bills.
- Look in the other corner, there is a pile of clothes.
- In the sink a pile of dishes, most of which are disposable.

The credits are rolling, and I know that soon REM will redeem me from this battle between consciousness and sleep. I am alive. The things that matter most to me are ok. My need to control is under control and is on break because all is well. I can try again tomorrow or not. I am all that I need to be in this moment.

Today is a perfect day.

The Serenity Prayer

God grant me the serenity to accept the things I cannot change, courage to change the things I can, and the wisdom to know the difference.

Serenity Prayer Remixed

God help me to stay sane. I need help not to remain a control freak. Help me to step back when others can handle it. Help me not to crack up because I did not do it, or redo it because I think there is a better way. Grant me peace, wisdom and sanity while learning the difference.

3. REMESSAGING WANDERINGS AND MUSINGS

"Everyone who wanders is not lost."
J.R.R. Tolkien

The name of this chapter is Wanderings and Musings. Sometimes having no direction is a direction. "Getting lost" may help point you in the right direction. Everything in life is not pointed or specific. Before proceeding to the next sections take the time now to wander and muse. Give yourself permission to let your mind and spirit soar to those places that are rarely nurtured or watered. There are no right or wrong answers here. Give yourself the gift of time, and discover something new and old about yourself. Give yourself credit for making it this far. Now give praise to God for making it this far. Take time and explore these journal questions.

☙

1. Pray/write a prayer that is truly from your heart. Be genuine expressing all of the inner you. Allow every experience, every emotion to be revealed. Prayer is the opportunity to be your most genuine self to a most genuine God.

_____
_____
_____

2. Considering the inventory of the author's life, how is yours the same? How is yours different. Take inventory of your life today. What is most important to you right now? How many things are important to you? List everything big and small.

_____
_____
_____
_____
_____

3. Is your list long or short, why do you think so? Is what you have listed something you focus on every day?

_____
_____
_____

4. How can you incorporate more things that are purposeful, fun, and self-preserving into what you are already doing?

_____
_____
_____

5. Children are among the wisest persons God ever invented. They help us to really consider and remind us how great God is and also make us aware of the true treasures in life. What are your thoughts about this?

    _____

    _____

    _____

6. What child in your life taught you a lesson?

    _____

    _____

    _____

7. What lesson was it?

    _____

    _____

    _____

8. How did it impact you?

    _____

    _____

    _____

9. What have you changed about yourself as a result of that lesson?

    _____

    _____

    _____

    _____

10.   If you can in your way, thank and honor that child by doing or plan something special with them today, and tell them how they helped you.

_____

_____

_____

11.   Are you doing what you want with your life?

_____

_____

_____

12.   If you are, congratulate yourself. Where do you see yourself next? If not, why?

_____

_____

_____

13.   Are you scared?

_____

_____

_____

14.   What questions haunt you?

_____

_____

_____

15.   Look at them. What does this fear look like or feel like to you? In other words, how have you let this fear manifest itself in your life?

_____

_____

_____

16.   How can you overcome it?

_____

_____

_____

17.   Who can you enlist to help in moving to the next level?

_____

_____

_____

18.   What does this fear represent?

_____

_____

_____

19.   Be honest, which is scarier, where you are today, or the thought of what would happen if do not do what your heart and spirit feels. Only you have the answers to the questions. Which of these two apply?

a. I am more scared of today.

b. I am more scared of not following my heart.

_____

_____

_____

20.   What does the perfect day look like to you? What would you have to do? What couldn't you do without? The perfect day looks like what to you?

_____

_____

_____

Now go and plan, play, explore and create the perfect day.

4. Self-Care

Intro to Self-Care

We are no good to others, if we are too depleted and too exhausted from providing them care and routinely neglecting yourself. It is extremely important that we learn to remessage that self -care means that you are being selfish. This simply is not true. Apply these simple flight instructions to your life. "Should the oxygen masks deploy, adults should breathe first, and then assist the children, seniors and others around you."

છે

Self-Care

Ms. Understood: You are a daughter, niece, sister, mother, aunt, cousin, friend and lover.

Ms. Understood: You are both strong and vulnerable, the best blend of femininity.

Ms. Understood: You were not designed to compete with or measure your value against the man.

Ms. Understood: You were made to share your views, offer advice and nurture the babies, yours and the ones entrusted to your care.

Ms. Understood: War is not your nature; unprovoked fighting goes against the core your foundation. That is unless your babies, your family and those you love are in jeopardy, or if there are threats to the home and space you have created.

Ms. Understood: Your dreams are not just for yourself, but also for the world.

Ms. Understood: God is for you even when you are not for yourself.

Ms. Understood: You do not have to apologize for being.

Ms. Understood: You have permission to change your mind, thus changing your world.

Dear Ms. Understood: If you unlock the secrets of living, loving and laughing, and you would have released you.

Ms. Understood: What I Never Knew I Wanted

Here's another way to think about life. Its problems, its transitions, its challenges, its victories, its summits, its valleys, its peaks, and the lessons we take away from each one of these experiences. This is everything I never knew I wanted.

Ms. Understood: Breath of God

Inhale.

Exhale.

Breathe in.

Deeply.

Breathe out.

Fully.

Take in fresh air.

Let out what God put on the inside of you.

Inhale.

Exhale.

When God made humanity, the definitive signal that all was well was the moment God breathed God's self into our humanity. At that moment, God breathed in God's self, God's total essence. Our bodies became enlivened and our spirits became emboldened. In an instant, we became both human and divine. In our purest state, our bodies and spirits are anxious to let loose all of the spirit of God in us. Inside the breath of God are creativity, order, foundation, compassion, love, and peace. The best way to honor the spirit of God that is in you is to release everything God has placed inside of you.

Ms. Understood, when you don't do whatever you know is your creative purpose that is as if you are holding your breath. As you go about your life do not forget to breathe. Exhale the characteristics of God. Those traits are the very reasons you were born. Your life is designed for you to find your purpose and to live in it. O_2 released is fresh air, but held in, it converts to a poison. And if you hold your breath too long, the air that is supposed to be expelled, will not assist you in living, but will assist in killing you. So that you may live fully in and on purpose, exhale the breath of God!

Ms. Understood: You Ain't the First, Only or Lonely

- You ain't the first. You ain't the only. You ain't the lonely.
- You ain't the first.
- Not the first to feel pain.
- Not the first to regret.
- Not the first to wonder what in your world is happening to you.
- Not the first to try and not have an available or accessible role model,
- The first, that's just how it feels.
- You ain't the only.
- Only one to feel stupid.
- Only one to make a mistake.
- Only one to start again.
- Only one to cry and not have a reason.
- Only one to cry for all the right or wrong reasons.
- Only, that's just how it feels.
- You ain't the lonely.
- Someone else felt out of place before you, and created room for you to move.
- Someone else doubted and still did it.
- Someone else didn't have a guide, or so they thought.
- Someone else triumphed in private and patted their own backs.
- Lonely, that's just how it feels.

Ms. Understood, if you could ever get over those feelings, you would be the first to know how terrific you really are, and that you are making it. And as soon as you know that, the world will know too and respond accordingly.

Ms. Understood: Get Some Help

Asking for help is sometimes viewed as a sign of weakness. One of the bravest things you could ever do is ask for help. Who says that you have to go it alone? Who says you must solve it by yourself? Who says no one wants to be bothered?

Probably the only person saying any of that is you. Life is not meant to be lived without the strength of others. It's funny how you will try. Oh sure, you don't mind jumping to another's rescue, but how difficult is it for you to receive what you so willingly parceled out? You couldn't stand it if someone rescued you, the way you rescued others.

You've shared. You've deposited good in the lives of others. How strange is it that you won't allow yourself to reap what you have sown? You've helped others, now it is your turn to accept assistance. That is how life works. Some days you are the giver. Some days you are the receiver. You cannot bear to harvest the goodness you have planted in the lives of others. Learn to become a receiver.

Don't know what to do?
> Ask somebody for help.

Don't know where you are?
> Ask somebody for help.

Don't know where to turn?
> Ask somebody for help.

Feeling Overwhelmed?
> Ask somebody for help.

Feeling crazy, lonely and hopeless?
> Ask somebody for help.

Are you in transition?
> Ask somebody for help.

Can't pray?
> Ask somebody for help.

Ms. Understood, there's nothing that you cannot ask help for. You don't have help, because you don't ask for help. When you ask for it; help is on the way! Reveal your strength in asking for help rather than not getting the help you need.

Ms. Understood: Just Say No

Can you?

No.

Will you?

No.

Only one more thing…

No.

There's just a little more,

No.

I see that you are tired but,

No.

Do you think you could?

No.

You said your plate is full but,

No.

Ms. Understood, no is a statement. No is a declaration. No does not have to be explained. No is understood. But No is not always accepted if it means, hold on, just this time or I'll try. People will get the wrong impression; if No does not mean No. No will not have density nor weight, if it sometimes means yes. My only job is to give No the full weight and authority it is supposed to carry. No is the first step towards self-care and is a preserver of mind, body and soul. No is the key to being ready to say yes. I will say No more often. No, I am not being selfish. I am self- preserving. No protects me. I cannot help you fully, if I am damaged and depleted from giving so much. No. No. No. No!

Ms. Understood: Who Loves You Baby?

Who loves you baby? Can you count yourself among the people who love you? Do you love you? Are you madly, sickly, head over heels geeked out about yourself? Would you hang out with you? Have you ever just told yourself, girl, not only do you have it going on, but, you have it going on! Are you the one somebody who loves you unconditionally, and with full acceptance of yourself? These are valid questions that deserve a closer look.

Bad eating.
No sleeping.
Fried foods with a side of fried foods.
All Pepsi's and no water, ever.
Is this the way you treat somebody you love?

Overextending yourself.
All taking and no giving.
All giving and no taking. Bad relationships.
Is this the way you treat somebody you love?

No vacations.
No exercise.
No spa days.
No new adventures.
Is this the way you treat somebody you love?

Negative songs.
Moodiness.
Mediocrity.
Sullen.
Brooding.

Short temper.

Is this the way you treat somebody you love?

Deferred Dreams.

Aborted Dreams.

Premature Dreams.

Is this the way you treat somebody you love?

Bad credit.

Late Bills.

All spending and no saving.

Is this the way you treat somebody you love?

Are you the one somebody you love? If you are, then why do you engage in behaviors that don't look or feel like someone in love? In most cases, the damage we do to ourselves is greater than most of the things that we suffer at the hands of others. If you are the somebody you love, doing better is always possible.

Ms. Understood, before anybody else can love you, you must love yourself deeply, richly, and unapologetically. Treat yourself the way you want to be treated. Do unto you, the way you want to be done unto. That way if no one ever does it for you, you cannot say that you were not treated well ever.

Ms. Understood: Enough

I am enough.

I am the right weight.

I am the right height.

I have the right shoe size.

I was born at the right time.

I was given the right life.

My parents were right for me.

My siblings were right for me.

My experiences were right for me.

My friends in all the seasons of my life were right for those times.

I prayed the right prayers.

I sung the right songs.

I lingered long enough.

I moved at the right time.

I learned enough.

I know enough.

All of these things combine to make me enough.

When I sit back and think about it I wouldn't change a thing.

If just one of these things changed, life would be so much different. I would be someone else, with other experiences, reflections, habits, curiosities and insights.

I would be another person and unable to affect those I am assigned to affect because just one thing about me changed.

Ms. Understood, some things I can change. I can become more of what I am, and if I never become more, for now at this moment I am enough.

Ms. Understood: I am Healed

You are healed from where you once hurt. It doesn't really hurt anymore. Sometimes you may forget that you outlasted something, because it now seems like child's folly. It is almost a distant memory, except there is a mark. There is an ugly scar that serves as a reminder, a badge of honor for the fight that you endured and ultimately won. Don't hide the scar; it marks the injury and reveals where it occurred. Don't cover it with it makeup. Don't hide it under layers of clothes. Don't embellish the story about its origins. Every scar has a story. Every tear has a testimony. Don't name it something else in order to hide where or how you obtained the scar. It is what it is.

There is a beauty in the scars we obtain in our spirits. The beauty is hidden and is within. The marks we bear prove to us that for every fight that leaves behind a blemish that there were healing powers within us. Those healing powers can only be exposed when the skin is broken. It is the only way that we truly know that you have everything that you have ever needed was always way down on the inside to heal you from where you once hurt.

Ms. Understood, touch where it once hurt, and rejoice because it no longer does.

5. REMESSAGING SELF-CARE

Women are nurturers by nature. We have an amazing capacity to give and care. Many of us will give and care to the point of exhaustion. Unfortunately, we are always the last on the list of receiving or accepting care. Self- care can be viewed as being selfish. The author believes that self- care is re-creation. Ever wonder why people live for the weekend, vacations or recreational activities. It is because it is the designated time for us to restore us. Re-creation is an important part of self- care. It is very important that we learn how to re-create, restore, and rediscover who we are. There are many ways to do so. Reading books like this. Prayer. Spa days. Dinner and a movie with your best friends are ways. It is very important to find and discover the many ways to recreate us. We are mind, body, spirit and soul. If any one of those areas is out balance, then we are out of balance. Our lifetimes must be spent finding ways to recreate each of those personas. Take time and journal this next set of questions.

&

1. Where/ when have you felt like the first, only or the lonely?

   _____

   _____

   _____

2. Do you allow yourself those feelings?

   _____

   _____

   _____

3. If you have overcome them, how do you feel now about yourself and where you were in that particular part of your life?

   _____

   _____

   _____

4. How do you take care of yourself?

   _____

   _____

   _____

5. In what ways do you take care of yourself?

   _____

   _____

   _____

6. Do you exercise?

_____

_____

_____

7. Do you eat well?

_____

_____

_____

8. Do you pray or meditate?

_____

_____

_____

9. Do you surround yourself with positive persons who fuel your dreams?

_____

_____

_____

10. Who are those people, and have you inspired each other recently? What is your inspiration?

_____

_____

_____

11. Are you currently involved in something where you could use a little help? What is it?

_____

_____

_____

12. Have you asked for help?

_____

_____

_____

13. What would it mean for you if you did?

_____

_____

_____

14. Who can help you the way that you have helped others?

_____

_____

_____

15. What kind of help do you need?

_____

_____

_____

16. Use of the word No is also a form of self-care. For some people, it can seem that saying No is being selfish, but the author believes that in some cases, it is actually self- preserving. What person, activity, or situation have you said yes to recently, and you needed to say no?

_____

_____

_____

17. Write your own statement for NO. Use it now, and save it for later.

_____

_____

_____

18. Everyone has an experience that seems insurmountable. In retrospect, what experiences have you overcome, that at one point you believed that you would never overcome. Are you healing (ed) from the experience?

_____

_____

_____

19. What does your healing look like?

_____

_____

_____

20. Using the table included name 10 things, traits, gifts that you believe that God has breathed into you, and name the ways you exhale (or share) your gifts to the world. Remember that when you share yourself with others, this is another way that you show self-care.

What God Inhaled in Me	What I Exhaled

6. DESTINY

Intro to Destiny

Destiny has planned for every caterpillar to become a butterfly. Whether or not a butterfly emerges depends on the actions of the caterpillar prior to the change. The process is difficult and slow, but the end is worth the journey. Instinctually, we all know that our lives are impactful and important. The tragedy is that sometimes we shy away from our greatness. This section focuses more on remessaging our day-to-day living. Remessaging helps us by calling forth glimpses of our future. We must continually tell ourselves that we will find, live in and enjoy that destiny.

∼

Destiny

Ms. Understood: The original thought.

(This is the first Ms. Understood note that I wrote to myself)

I am who I am.

I will do what I do.

Because now I understand, the greatest tragedy of life is not to be who I am.

Who can do what you do the way you do, how you do, why you do, but you?

Ms. Understood, There's nobody but you.

Ms. Understood: Go There

Let me go There.

You feel different? You don't fit in? There is something askew? Well, if you feel out of sorts, if you feel out of place, it is because you are out of place. You are in the wrong place.

Here is not where you are supposed to be. Here was just supposed to be a pit stop, but you have made it a home. Your living quarters are becoming tight and confining. Your mind and heart knows there is another place for you, but you stay Here.

Leave Here. Why stay Here? Why not go There? If you go There it will be different, it is the change you are looking for. It is the change you need to fulfill your destiny.

So what about There? There is Here with a T.

- Fit you to a T.
- Suit you to a T.
- Made to a T.

Have you ever heard someone say don't go There with me. Or has someone ever asked why would you go There?

But maybe you should ask yourself this. Why not go There? You haven't been There, before. You know about Here. And something inside lets you know that Here is not where you want to be. Here is safety. Here is familiar. Here is known.

But There is where you will fit. There is where you will thrive. There is waiting patiently for your arrival. Over There is Over Here. You will soon be over Here, if you go There. When you move, then you will not be Here any more.

Are you ready to go There?

Ms. Understood: About Coming Attractions

Your whole life you have flirted with your destiny. It seems to be a series of missed opportunities or a series of false starts, or rather is it a series of coming attractions? Can you really say for sure that you were ready for all that was coming? Think back and be honest with yourself. Had you been thrust into the opportunity, you may have aborted the mission, because you did not have all the right stuff. You would have suffered from premature maturation. Like a teenage girl, you have all the working parts; you have the look of a woman, the sound of a woman, but not the fortitude, insight, patience or presence of a woman.

Chances are you would have gotten in the room and done well by outsiders standards, but something on the inside of you would have known that you could have given more, made a greater impact if you would have waited. Waited for your essence to become full. It has been said that your gifts can lead you where your character cannot keep you.

Don't fret; you are not a victim of mediocrity, although that is a feeling that can certainly cause doubt in you. You have been divinely pre-positioned to wait. Waiting sucks doesn't it? I would agree with you. But while you are waiting, you are changing, your spirit is becoming convinced of what God innately placed in you, your creativity is flourishing. Tell the truth when the opportunity previously presented itself, you were not quite ready. You were ready in the sense that you needed to encounter and glimpse at what would one day become ordinary for you. The near misses are divine encounters. There are some things you've got to see for yourself, sense for yourself; hence, the near misses. This is why it hurts so badly, when it feels like a missed opportunity. Divine waiting is orchestrated to invade your curiosity, which produces an unrest in you that hastens you to prepare yourself, to steady your resolve, to hone your craft, and find the haughtiness of your spirit, so that the next time, and there will be a next time, you will be ready, full and complete, and knowing, that you have given the world the very best of your God given self. This waiting is like a movie preview, or a coming attraction.

Coming attractions only give you a clue that the movie (your life) is nearly ready and available for your consumption. Coming attractions whet your appetite. All the elements are there, you are slightly aware of the beginning, the plot, the main characters, you see the setting, you see some of the highlights, and the special effects. Yes, all the elements are there all right, there is even a hint of the dialogue. You don't know the middle, and you can only guess at the ending. But what you know for sure is whether or not you want to participate. You know even then whether or not you are ready to risk the purchase of the ticket, based on the preview.

Ms. Understood: About Walking

You are able bodied; have functioning legs; and have already mastered one of the greatest and most difficult challenges of your life… that is learning to walk. That's right walking. Go back to your earliest lessons in walking. In learning to walk, children sometimes fall. Those falls are called mistakes. Children do not see it as that, even though that is what it is. Those mistakes cause tears, tantrums, awkward movements and the bruising of young egos. But the failure to walk right away creates a drive that is insatiable to finally master the task. The process of learning to walk yields multiple results. The process strengthens legs, butts and resolves. Everyday a child cannot walk; brings that child closer to the day and moment when they can. In the interim, other changes occur, their crawling pace is increased, their legs are strengthened; they become aware of the places and the people where there is help. Until one day they walk.

The object of walking is not learning to fall, but it is learning to walk. And when you learn to walk, it is not called learning to fall. It is called learning to walk. Walk with your head held high, reaching for hands to hold and guide. Walk unsure of your steps. Walk strengthening your steps and your resolve.

Ms. Understood, that much falling inevitably creates great walkers. Fall with grace; walk with strength.

Ms. Understood: About Mistakes

How can you not appreciate your mistakes? I mean really. Your mistakes are the stuff legends are made of. The most humorous stories about yourself have to do with you and your so- called mistakes. Sometimes, people can make you feel really badly because you make them. Like they don't have any. More than that, you can make yourself feel badly about your mistakes. Mistakes bleed of imperfections and expose vulnerabilities. Vulnerabilities are not what we want to show others, but they are certainly what most people will see before they see our ideas of perfection for ourselves. Chances are they won't view them the same way you see it, but I digress. Life is more about learning from and through mistakes. Without them, how else would you learn? How else would you know? How else would you be able to laugh at yourself or measure your progress?

From time to time, some mistakes are happy accidents. What about when you took the wrong turn and found that fabulous shoe store or restaurant that is now a favorite getaway? What about when you inadvertently threw away the phone number to the cute guy and kept the number to the other guy who didn't look as exciting? You called him and it's a year later, can you even imagine your life without him? You thought you were visiting the church of your friend, but heard the right message at the right time at the "wrong church." Was it a mistake, or just what you needed?

Some mistakes are harmless, affecting no one but you. Some are painful, having repercussions for years. Now here is word of caution and distinction. Repetition of the same error in succession is not a mistake, that is willful stubbornness to learn on your part; and there is a difference. The recovery time from every mistake varies; largely due to the fact that you made mistakes before. The more mistakes you make, the less often you make them. How ironic and inspiring at the same time.

A mistake = a missed take on a problem. You saw it one way and settled on a solution you thought would work; but it revealed itself as something else altogether, and either your solution was improbable or impossible. Ultimately and accidentally, you find another solution. You find the right solution for that time. A mistake is having partial knowledge coupled with unknown factors. Don't hate your mistakes, or feel that they are unrecoverable. Our mistakes can become effective tools. Mistakes are past inhibitions for future inspirations.

Ms. Understood that inherently packaged in every mistake is the same life lesson. Learn. Recover. Journey.

Ms. Understood: Why not Today?

Today is as good as any to get things started. You know what things to do. You have been fixated on them a long time. It is not a hobby; it is not something that does not need a whole lot of attention. It is your passion. Passionate things do not die. When left unattended, passionate things, smolder, the embers do not burst into flames, but their heat becomes contained and intensifies. You can't get it out of your head. Your passion ignites your soul. Your destiny waits patiently for you to decide to finally embrace it.

Why not today? Why not now? How many Mondays have passed for you to say, tomorrow? And then when tomorrow comes, nothing? Mondays elongate into weeks. The weeks, well now, they have added up. How many months have been immersed into years gone by? How long will you delay your own dreams? How long will you set aside your ambitions for deadlines you care less about, projects that will not yield you full recognition, committees and monuments of nothingness? Before your years disappear into your lifetime, and you are no longer; come on, do something with today. I am not saying accomplish it all today. That's impossible. What's inside of you is the idea of a lifetime. Nope, you don't have to think it all today. Just get it started. Make progress. Do not get it perfect. Get it going. Get it outside your head and heart, and get it into someone else's head and heart.

Ms. Understood, in your mind's eye it already is. So make it so.

Ms. Understood: Perception is Reality

As a child, one of the worst things about going to bed at night was the boogey man. No matter how safe and secure you were. No matter how fresh you felt after your evening bubble bath; no matter how tranquil your bedtime story or sincere your bedtime prayer, there was always the threat of the boogey man. No matter that you knew your parents were just down the hall. No matter that you had faced the battle the night before, the boogey man loomed and was waiting to commence with the nightly battle. You had to face it alone, or so you thought.

Wasn't it amazing that as soon as you yelled to your parents to hold you, to rescue you and to calm you they so did effortlessly, with a flick of the switch? All was cured as soon as they turned on the light. The presence of the boogeyman disappeared under the illumination and returned with the absence of the light.

Light on. Light off. Light on, everything is ok. Light off, shadows. Light on, security. Light off, evil persona. Light on, the boogey man was all gone. Nothing in the room has changed. Nothing about you has changed. The time of day has not changed. The only change is the light. But what a difference the light makes.

With a little light; even just a night light, the boogey man was noticeably smaller. No wonder we concentrated on that little light until our eyes grew heavy with sleep. With the big light on, the boogey man was assassinated mercilessly and sleep would lovingly overtake us, as it should in the night.

It would be weeks, and maybe months of torturous visions before you understood that the light is what made the boogey man dissipate, and darkness dispel. Small wonder that we forget that key lesson from childhood. As we age and master the boogey man of our childhood, somehow we miss the metamorphosis about that specter. It grows up too. In a way, it still exists.

It just has a different form. Now it looks like insecurity, doubt, intimidation, self-pity, low self-esteem, or angst in new situations.

How are you looking at what you are looking at? For someone looking on the outside, what you are facing now looks like the opportunity of the century. But does it look the same for you? How you view yourself, your situations, and your immediate concerns will either give life or death to the boogey man. If you see it as bad and unable to resolve, that's what it will be. But if you see it as a teaching moment with some extra tough moments, then that is what it will be. Perception is reality.

Ms. Understood, the remedy for the boogey man is still the same, just turn on the light. Turn on the light gained from your mistakes. Turn on the light from your friends. Turn on the light of your inner self, what you know is right for you to do right now. Turn on the light. Turn on the light of God, be guided, be sure, and be firm knowing that God knows what God is doing in your life. Kill the boogey man; change your perception. See it differently. A change in your perception is a change in you. Today it looks like the boogey man. Tomorrow it will become the best thing that has ever happened to you.

Ms. Understood: About Courage

What does courage look like on any day? Doubt. Fear. Intimidation. Indecision. Cautious. Hesitation. Faithless. Dread. Apprehension. Sorrow. Suffering.

Courage rarely looks like itself up close. Courage generally clothes itself in some pretty awful stuff. Only later does it look like a designer original, and becomes the thing that is envied and desired of others.

Remind yourself, if you are scared, you are most likely being courageous.

If you are cautious, and moving forward, yes it is probably courage.

If you feel as if every movement is a mistake and it is because you are in a situation that you have never been in before, yes, you are being courageous.

Are you doing something new? Are you doing something different? That's courage. You are now in the category of phenomenal people who affect the world.

You will be counted among the lesser known and the greater known of this world.

I imagine that there are many courageous people in the world, some famous, some not. But in doing what they did. I doubt courage is what any of them felt. Courage is the name we give it, after they accomplish and complete a seemingly insurmountable goal. But if you don't know, you better ask somebody!

- Ask Oprah about moving from Tennessee to Baltimore.
- Ask Sojourner Truth about addressing a predominately white abolitionist group.
- Ask Zora Neale Hurston about writing about love the way she knew it could be, and the way it really was.
- Ask Harriet Tubman about coming back the first time, after she's already garnered her own freedom.

- Ask Eve about eating the forbidden fruit and living 900 more years after the fact.

- Ask Esther about seeing the King on behalf of her people.

- Ask the woman with the issue of blood about reaching out for Jesus.

- Ask your momma about the first pains of labor with you or her first pregnancy.

- Ask The Little Rock Nine.

- Ask the mother who confronts the drug pushers on her block for the sake of not just hers, but your children as well.

- Ask the Haitian or Cuban refugees who only have a rubber placement separating them from the Atlantic Ocean and a watery grave.

- Ask the woman who returns to school after raising her children.

- Ask the ex-offender who must explain the gaps in her employment history.

- Ask the divorcee who opens a practice because she wants to help others like herself.

- Ask the woman who wears white after Labor Day.

- Ask the woman who sings Aretha's songs loudly, but sounds like Moms Mabley.

- Ask the battered woman who escapes under the cover of night.

- Ask the homosexual who openly displays love for her partner.

- Ask the woman who applies for welfare after being downsized from her job in management.

- Ask the career professional who leaves her job and then lives on her retirement until her passion can profit her.

- Ask the person in therapy risking her reputation to receive the treatment that is needed to battle clinical depression and anxiety.

Ms. Understood, there is a greater fear than not being courageous; not heeding the call that is the purpose of your life, and that fear is regret. So many are courageous, and you are among them.

7. REMESSAGING DESTINY

"People often meet their destiny on the road they take to avoid it."
French Proverb

Destiny is what we are here on earth to achieve. It is the one question on earth that no one can answer but you. And here is the catch. The answer is somewhere deep inside of you. And it takes genuine work to find it. But it can be found! There are so many books in the market about purpose and destiny. Many authors write about how, when and why we should locate our destiny. Despite the methodology of discovering destiny, whether it's through religion, meditation or self-reflection, most writers agree on one thing. If you don't find your destiny, life basically has no real meaning. There is a greater something that we are designed for. This chapter is not so much an attempt for me to advise as to how to find that destiny, other than to say that you have to continually call it forth. The author believes that you must challenge where you are at this present moment. It is imperative that you continue to speak to yourself, and speak to your circumstances. There is no right or wrong way to find it. What I know is if you continue to search for it, you will arrive there. But again, you must call it forth. To reveal your destiny, you must challenge your perceptions, challenge yourself and the beliefs that hold you back, summon your courage, ask yourself what in the world you are doing, and finally you must create a vision of the world you want, then work towards it. I believe that when we make the effort to uncover our destiny, we will arrive at the destination that God always intended for us.

1. Take time in this space and create a vision of the life you want. You know the beginning, you are living the middle and the end is up to you. Now write a coming attraction of that vision: In a world where everything was as it should be in my life,

_____

_____

_____

_____

_____

_____

_____

_____

_____

_____

_____

_____

_____

2. Fear comes in many forms and is one of the biggest boogey men of them all. What is your boogey man, what can you do to shed light on it? My boogey man is in the form of :

_____

_____

_____

_____

_____

_____

3. The light I will shed on the problem is:
   a.　　The light of_____
   b.　　The light of _____
   c.　　The light of _____
   d.　　The light of_____

4. There is Here with a T. Let yourself go There. What does Here look like for you?

   _____
   _____
   _____
   _____
   _____
   _____

5. Is your Here representative of your most optimal state, yes or no and why or why not?

   _____
   _____
   _____
   _____

6. Is this the year to go There? If not, then when is it? Please name the year, or moment you will finally get started?

   _____
   _____
   _____
   _____

7. What feelings do you associate with Here? What feelings do you assign to There? Of the two, which feelings would you rather have? Which life would you rather have? Here or There? Take a sheet of paper, split it into two columns. Label one column Here, then label the other column There. State the differences between the two places, really describe how each looks to you. Finally, how do you plan to pursue your choice?

_____

_____

_____

_____

_____

8. Will your choice be your optimal self, and does that choice place you on the path to your ultimate destiny?

_____

_____

_____

_____

_____

_____

9. Courage does not look itself up close. When you were having a courageous moment, what did it feel like when you initially experienced it?

_____

_____

_____

_____

_____

10. Where have you been courageous in your life? I acknowledge that I showed courage when I did what?

_____

_____

_____

_____

_____

_____

11. Recall some of your happy mistakes. Who, where or what did you discover during that time?

_____

_____

_____

_____

_____

_____

12. Recall some of your worst mistakes in your life. How has it made you better?

_____

_____

_____

_____

_____

_____

_____

13. What did you learn about yourself that you otherwise you would not have learned had you not made the mistake?

_____

_____

_____

_____

_____

_____

14. A television slogan advises us to make progress every day. So if you cannot make big steps, how about baby steps? Remember the author included her very first Ms. Understood within this chapter. It was not a lengthy entry. But the original thought became a book. Why not today? If today is your last day on the job, and you knew that all of your needs would be met tomorrow, how would you then explore your destiny? Answer the following truthfully:

a. I most want to pursue:

_____

_____

_____

b. In the final stage, it looks like:

_____

_____

_____

_____

_____

15. These are the baby steps towards my goal:

a. _____

b. _____

c. _____

d. _____

e. _____

Here's an example:

- I want to be a public speaker. In the final stage, it looks like my calendar will be filled with speaking events.
- A baby step towards my goal is to speak to some young ladies at a workshop about achieving goals.

8. CONVERSATION

Intro to Conversation

This section will be devoted to what you are telling you. If what you are saying to yourself is not helpful or beneficial then work must begin on altering your self-talk. Some of the most important conversations we have are with our internal selves and the subsequent dialogue with the Eternal. Think of your life as one long conversation between you and God. Think of what the conversation is like. God keeps telling you to expect the best, because you are the best, because God has selected the best for you. And imagine that every time God talked to you, you responded with negativity, doubt and insecurity. Liberate your language, change the conversation you are having with yourself. Then adapt to the language the Creator is speaking inside of you, repeat the Creator's affirmation of you, by living out loud, unapologetic and free.

&

Conversation

God: "You're the best."

You: " No I am the worst."

God: " There is no like you, you are unique."

You: "No there's nothing special about me."

Imagine how many ways and times God tries to get you to say what God has always been saying about you. Who is a more compelling witness, a God that knows everything or you who is guessing along the way?

Ms. Understood, remessaging conversation is the most difficult and rewarding inward task. But once you change your talk, you will change you, and everything falls into place.

Ms. Understood: Practice Makes Perfect

Practice makes perfect. If you do something long enough, you will perfect it.

When you said you couldn't, you didn't.

When you spoke doubt, you didn't.

When you were faithless, you failed.

When you hesitated, your dreams were halted.

When you practiced negativity and doubt that is exactly what you got.

You perfected sabotage. You have perfected withholding yourself from yourself and the world. You perfected shrinking. And you got more than you bargained for. You did not bargain for indecision and being caught in a state of liminality. But that is the result of perfecting doubt and indecision.

Change your language, gradually, slowly, and gently. You will meet yourself with resistance. After all, you have perfected the language that has bound you, and the language of hope, of freedom, of destiny is nascent, embryonic, and burgeoning. It does not have the strength and skill that your former tongue has perfected. With repetition and practice and yes, even more practice you will develop the language and the mindset that will free and unchain your life.

Your new language of hope sounds funny doesn't it?

Practice. Practice. Practice.

Keep speaking; learn how to form the words with your mouth.

Practice. Practice. Practice.

Put them in the air; let them linger in the atmosphere.

Practice. Practice. Practice.

Practice makes perfect. If you do something long enough, you will perfect it.

Tell yourself you can do it. It sounds strange. You can do it all. You may not be able to do it all at once, but it all can get done. Like the age-old question asks, how does one eat an elephant? Take one bite at a time.

Ms. Understood that practice makes perfect. If you do something long enough, you will perfect it.

Ms. Understood: Mantras

There are phrases that we rehearse until they become grafted to our mind like DNA in our skin. These words, phrases, beliefs both spoken and not are our mantras. Mantras are the clarion call of the soul. You are identified by what you say and how often you say it. So what are you saying about yourself now? Some of it does not bear repeating. Trash it. Let's do it new. Out with the old and in with the new. You don't have to wait until the beginning of the year for this transition. Out with resolutions, start a revolution... in you. If I continue to hold to these old thoughts, these old mantras, catch phrases of my soul, then I would inevitably be stuck. I mean this stuff just doesn't work anymore. Since I am changing, then what I am saying should change. Old mantras in new journeys hurt your progress. Continue thinking like this, and you will be like a pillar of worthless salt stuck holding things of former value, looking back and within the reach of safety. There are some things you have got to let go of.

Ms. Understood that mantra changing is a process, and a massive undertaking, but with time and consistency, I'll replace the old with the new.

My Old Mantras:

- I need to be in control.
- I am not good enough.
- I must be perfect.
- I am a fraud and will be exposed as such.
- Settle.
- Enough is not adequate, you must do more.
- You don't deserve to be loved as you are.
- I'm just not good enough; therefore I am disqualified.
- I am not lovable, so I will perform well to become likeable.

- No one knows or understands what I am going through. I am alone.

My New Mantras

- Perfection is not attainable, however, completion is always possible.
- It's just as easy to believe the good about you, as it is to believe the bad about you.
- Believe it when your friends say they need you.
- You really do matter.
- When you take care of yourself, you'll be strong enough to take care of others.
- Stuff. Mess. Sugar, Honey, Iced Tea... awwww shut my mouth... sure does happen. And there are only ever two choices; sit in it or clean it up!
- Face it you are blessed.
- You have been given the breath of God, exhale.
- If it doesn't change today, it will be changed.
- I am the one person who ensures that I can be happy. I will not give that power away.

Ms. Understood: Watch Your Mouth

Watch your mouth! Watch what you say! If you can't say the right thing, at least; keep your mouth shut. Be quiet, until you can say it better.

When you speak negatively, that is exactly what you get. Did you ever wake up and say I feel like today is going to be a good day? Not as often as you said, I think I am going to have a bad day. And whenever you said it; that is exactly what happened. Everything unimaginable seems to attract itself to you until you finally are able to go to sleep. What about when you said, nothing exciting ever happens to me? You got a great big fat heaping dose of nothingness, with a side order of boring nothingness. You will attract exactly what you say. What about I am broke? Well, as long as you say that your bank account is nebulous. If you said you were going to be late, or that the traffic was not going to agree with you, or you thought your supervisor would call you in to the office, or that your meal would be ruined, or that the guy would never call, your child was a bad seed, or prepared for a speech that you said would not be good, what happened? Exactly what you said. Do you think that it is a coincidence that you have been able to catalogue more bad than good? That is because you have spoken more about the bad than the good. And then you don't have the good sense to stop giving life to the bad, because you rehearse and give it strength that it would not otherwise have, unless you continued to speak to it.

When you speak hope, your circumstance has an opportunity to reveal itself. When you speak faith, your situation will later have the evidence of what you imagined in your heart and believed in your spirit. When you speak in love, you will have unleashed the greatest single weapon against any wrong in the world. Life is in the power of the tongue. Words have life. Words are the singular germinating influence of this world. The things in this world that are remarkable, useful and necessary all started with a thought; that became a spoken edict. Someone said: A man can fly. My children will matter in this world. I can be better than I am. I am not defined by my past. I am the bravest. I am the strongest. I am the best. I will change. I will grow. I will overcome.

Life is in the power of the tongue. God spoke the very existence of the world and all things in it in to being. And if we are made in God's image, and we are, God has given us the same ability to speak and to order, shape and define our worlds. At the conclusion of creation, God spoke and said it was good. Can you say the same of the world you have spoken into existence? Our words are efficacious whether we speak life or we speak death. Speak life.

Take your mouth off yourself. Learn how to speak differently. Every self -defeating remark is a prescription for misery. Do you really want to go through this whole life miserable?

Ms. Understood, until you learn, relearn and master the power of your tongue, shut up and watch your mouth.

Ms. Understood: About Minimizing

You have the right to remain silent. You also have the right to boast loudly, about you!

"All I did was" has become semi profane, in a martyr me kind of way. You can measure your self-worth almost by the number of times you repeat the phrase All I did was… Inevitably, you won't feel so great about yourself, because you have chosen to diminish all the good you have done. What has led you to feeling unappreciated by others is the fact that you have never appreciated yourself. Others cannot appreciate you if you have not taught them how to treat you or what kind and form of appreciation you value. Somewhere someone erroneously led you to believe that it was better that you don't toot your own horn, and to remain silent. Gratitude and appreciation of yourself only comes when you let it out. They said it is boastful. They said it demeans others. By saying what you did you in fact advertises that you are able to make situations better, livable, and bearable. It announces your place in humanity.

Minimizing your daily life is not fair to you. What you view as ordinary and uneventful has impact. Believe it. All you did, is who you are. It has meaning. Fortunately, you are not the only authority on you. Ask the people whose lives you have impacted, by all that you've done.

All I did was wash the dishes. All I did was the laundry. All I did was cook dinner. All I did was clean the room. All I did was sit with my friend while she cried. All I did was take the kids to the park. All I did was graduate from high school. All I did was my job well. All I did was graduate from college. All I did was show up. All I did was drive her over there. All I did was pick him up when it was over. All I did was sing. All I did was preach. All I did was give of my time, my talent, and my treasure.

Remessaging All I did becomes this: All I did was live. All I did was affect a life. All I did was leave a lasting imprint. All I did was provide stability. All I did was have impact. All I did was make a memory. All I did was be the best human being I was capable of being. All I did was secure a future for myself. All I did was use my time wisely. All I did was teach a child to love and respect others. All I did was what I could and that became enough to answer someone's prayers. When did what you do not become enough? What would the results have been had you done nothing, not been available and not been willing. You would shudder to think right? And so would the people who are the recipients of All I did was.

Ms. Understood, give you yourself credit. Maximize all you did. Think about what you did. No really do it. All you did was care, and that is a lot.

Ms. Understood: About Measuring Up

You are wonderfully and fearfully made. You are already the bomb. You are it. One of the hardest things to do is to believe that you are already adequate and that you are already equipped. You are already good enough. Isn't that hard enough to believe? You don't have to do another thing. You are good enough. There are no standards to measure up to. Comparing yourself to others is at best, a wasted effort.

Somewhere inside of you there is a piece of you that really, really knows that the only thing that you can do is to improve upon perfection. God has never made a mistake. And God didn't make one when you were created. When God released you upon the earth, the timing, the people, and your experiences were all part of the grand stage set for your arrival. Trust that a loving, affirming, forgiving hand, has guided you. And all along that hand leads you to the place where you will shine the brightest.

What is average for you is extraordinary for others. If what you are capable of were placed in someone else's hand, they would struggle and mishandle the same task. You are unique! It seems average to you because it is what you were specifically designed to do. Stop holding yourself back waiting for a better version of you to emerge before you try to do what you have been equipped to accomplish. Good enough is good enough indeed! Have you wondered why those ideas come to you so effortlessly, almost as fluid as breathing? It is the essence of you. You gifts are a part of your DNA. They are as much a part of you as your subatomic structure and the follicles of your hair. You just can't help yourself! You do what you do, because you are who you are.

There is no need to compare yourself to another. There is no need to measure your experiences, gifts, talents, or life against another's. A Van Gogh, a Steinway, or a Faberge Egg is esteemed because of their rarity, precision in design and value assigned to them.

And even though their creators have designed other works to consider, their beauty, sound and quality are measured individually. Each has value standing alone, and as a part of a collection. When God created the whole of humanity, He had no need to create another one like you, because everything about you was just right, adequate, and sufficient. If you believe that God does everything with precision, then what do you believe about yourself?

Ms. Understood: You completely measure up. The Creator values you. When you get out of your way, you will have immeasurable benefit to yourself and immeasurable benefit to the world.

Ms. Understood: You are Wonderful

Words cannot define you. Words cannot capture your essence. They can merely hint at the greatness inside. You are uniquely you. Nobody else is you. You are a one of a kind original, especially crafted and designed by God. Much of your time and energy has been devoted to thinking about what someone said about you and what you thought they said about you. Too often what you remember was not helpful, but hurtful. You over accomplished, over achieved, and over did it so that you could hear someone say something different about you, so that you could hear the right words that would make you feel ok about yourself.

Ms. Understood, that you do need someone to affirm you. YOU. You are that person. Look at yourself in the mirror, go ahead and look. That is the one person, that can tell you what you need to hear, exactly when you need to hear it, and you can say it as many times as you need to hear it. You are the only person who knows all about you. You are the only person, who will accompany you on the entire journey called your life. You can pinpoint the words and phrased that have hurt you, torn you down, made you feel less than. But words also can build you up, and fortify your resolve.

Words are life. Don't you want to live? Aren't you tired of the caustic effects of bad words? Don't you want to live uninhibited, and unrestrained by the limits of words on your life? Somehow you have embraced and hang onto to the words that have destroyed you. Let's not do that anymore. It's ok, talk to yourself. Tell yourself, Girl you have got it going on. You have IT! You are the bomb-diggity. You are a force of nature. Live, knowing that you are a part of the plan, the grand design, the whole scheme of things, you matter.

I am not asking you to believe it all right now. That may be too hard. But you are strong enough just to say them. Put the words in the air that affirm you, convince and compel you. Say the words that will heal and help. You say, that you don't have any words, here are few to hang your hat on. Let them float into the atmosphere and trickle into your soul like a fine mist early in the morning. Live, knowing that you are:

Captivating, attractive, appealing, enticing, enthralling, fascinating, fabulous, magnificent, remarkable, great, superb, amazing, breathtaking, astonishing, fantastic, brilliant, tremendous, marvelous, extraordinary, peculiar, uncommon, rare, unusual, special, exceptional, singular, notable, outstanding, noteworthy, admirable, astonishing, astounding, awe-inspiring, awesome, brilliant, cool, divine, dynamite, enjoyable, excellent, extraordinary, fabulous, fantastic, fine, groovy, incredible, magnificent, marvelous, miraculous, outstanding, peachy, phenomenal, pleasant, pleasing, prime, remarkable, sensational, something else, staggering,, stupendous, super, superb, surprising, swell, terrific, too much, tremendous, unheard-of, wondrous, adventurous, audacious, confident, courageous, daring, dashing, dauntless, defiant, fearless, firm, forward, gritty, gutsy, hardy, heroic, indomitable, intrepid, lionhearted, nervy, plucky, resolute, spirited, spunky, stalwart, strong, unabashed, unafraid, undaunted, undismayed, unfearful, valiant, adventuresome, attractive, best ever, cat's pajamas, choice, commendable, cool, copacetic, deserving, dream, estimable, excellent, exquisite, fine, gnarly, good, great, greatest, groovy, hunky dory, laudable, meritorious, neat, peachy, praiseworthy, rare, smashing, solid, spiffy, super, super-duper, superior, unreal, valuable, worthy, awesome, astonishing, awe-inspiring, beautiful, breathtaking, far out, formidable, grand, imposing, impressive, magnificent, majestic, mind-blowing, moving, striking, stunning, wondrous, cool, accomplished, able, adept, adequate, adroit, alert, bright, capable, competent, cunning, dexterous, endowed, equipped, good, admirable, attractive, capital, champion, choicest, desirable, distinctive, distinguished, exceptional, exemplary, exquisite, fine, first-class, first-rate, good, great, incomparable, invaluable, magnificent, meritorious, notable, noted, outstanding, premium, priceless, prime, skillful, striking, superb, superlative, supreme, tiptop, top-notch, transcendent, intelligent, knowing, powerful, qualified, ready, smart, strong, and worthy.

Ms. Understood know that you are absolutely wonderful!

Ms. Understood: Mentoring

Be a mentor. In helping somebody, you will help yourself. By teaching others you will discover that somewhere along the way you learned something. You have achieved something. You have successfully mastered an area where you once struggled. Because of your experiences, there is a grace about you where others will flounder.

Be a mentor. Do not have someone become your clone; after all there is only one you. Mentor, challenge, compel, and transform those who allow your stories to impact them. No one can know that they can make it, achieve, get over it, get through, or get by if you continue to remain silent about your past. As you mentor, you will discover how rich, filling, and deep your story truly is. As you share, you will become transformed by your experiences again. The pain, regret, and shame that you initially felt will subside, you will be able to recount your history with less pain, and more gratitude for God allowing it. Through your mentee's eyes, you will see that God allowed the experience for instructions and wisdom to impart. What once hurt, can heal more persons than yourself.

Be a mentor. You do not serve you or humanity well if you don't testify. Tell your story, the whole story. Don't leave out any details. Talk about the happy and the flowery along with the gory details that make for great epics. But then do more than tell the story. Help guide someone through their story, through their journey. This is the duty of a mentor: to shepherd, to disciple and to love indescribably and unabashedly. Love with advice, critique and most of all care. Here's the part you may not like; don't offer your opinion, or tell them "honey child if it was me I would..." Nope that doesn't help. What helps is if you remain a steady force; acknowledge the choices that are available to your mentee and lovingly and skillfully draw out of them what is innately in them; as it was drawn out of you. Remember you made your own choices, and your choices led to the story that you are able to share. It's one great big circle of learning.

Ms. Understood that you should be a mentor. Don't wait, until you have a perfect notion of what a mentor is. Impart, teach, encourage while on your journey. You will be surprised at what you will learn again, and you will understand that you will not always be a student, but have become a master.

Ms. Understood: About You

You. Imperfect. You. Flawed. You. With experiences. You with regrets. You with fear. You. With the crooked smile. You with the hairstyle hiccups. You without the high-school body. You. Having failed, but overcome. You. Having made mistakes, but shares how to avoid the land mines. You. The one who cries privately, but openly cares. You. Friend to many, lonely to self. The giver. You. The listener. You. Who may offend, but apologizes. You. Who does more good, than bad. You. Who extends self, body, mind and soul. You. Who tries again and again. You. No longer the victim. You. Seeker of truth. You. The rebounder. You the starter. You. The finisher. You. The achiever. You. With wisdom. You. Lover of life. Out the box, pushing the boundaries and the one uniquely designed, if but only for one other you along the journey. You. Matter. You. Are needed. You are the one who the world has been waiting for. Be you. Embrace you. Love you. Live you.

Hey God,

Yes, daughter.

Where are you?

Where I've always been.

Oh... I was just checking. By the way, thanks.

For what?

Everything.

The trials too?

Yup, those too.

You are welcome.

9. REMESSAGING CONVERSATION

Out of the mouth, flow the issues of life.

What you are talking about, when you talk about you? The most influential conversations you will have during your life will be the ones you have with yourself. These conversations will weigh heavily as you make decisions about your life, ranging from the smallest to the largest. What we say and how we say it shapes who we ultimately become. Words have life. Our lives, insights, and outcomes are a direct reflection of our internal talk. Remember that your life is a lifelong conversation between you and God. Shouldn't some of that talk be happy, inspired and carefree? Here is your opportunity to explore your conversation with yourself in more detail.

ॐ

1.   What is the one affirmation that you need to hear often? Write it down and tell this to yourself right now.

_____

_____

2.   What are some of the old mantras that you clung to? If they were destructive how will you rewrite them so that they support who you are right now, as a progressing, healing woman. Below are two columns. We've done this before; list your Old Mantras on one side and your New Mantras on the other.

Old Mantras	New Mantras

3. Do you remember the section on all I did was? Have you ever minimized something you did? Are you a regular minimizer? Name five things that you have done when you said, "all I did was."

   a. _____
   b. _____
   c. _____
   d. _____

4. Call or find people who directly benefited from all I did was? Ask them to tell you what it meant to them, listen carefully and absorb and embrace their words realizing that you have impact and importance in this world. Write notes on the experience.

   _____
   _____
   _____
   _____
   _____
   _____

5. Who benefited?

   _____
   _____
   _____
   _____
   _____
   _____

6. What did they say was the result of your selfless actions?

_____

_____

_____

_____

_____

_____

7. You are absolutely wonderful. The author included hundreds of adjectives to describe how great you are. In the space below, rewrite at least 25 of the adjectives that you connected with. Say them as you write them.

_____

_____

_____

_____

_____

_____

Now that you have seen what remessaging looks like and how it can sound, write yourself some Ms. Understood notes. Let the last words in the book be the ones you write or think. Happy discovery and God bless!

a. _____

b. _____

c. _____

d._____

ABOUT THE AUTHOR

Kimberly Taylor is a talented and gifted author, musician, and minister. She has obtained a Bachelor's Degree from James Madison University and her Masters of Divinity from Howard University School of Divinity. She has nearly 20 years professional ministry experience. Her vocational career also illustrates her capacity to provide quality care, professionally she has worked as a counselor, probation officer, and program manager for a non –profit. In addition to preaching, Ms. Taylor has had the privilege to serve as a lecturer, seminar presenter, and conference host. In her spare time, Ms. Taylor lives for the extraordinary in the ordinary days with her godchildren, nieces and nephews. She simply adores life now because she actually got through her 'doozie.' This is her premiere publication. Ms. Taylor resides in Metropolitan Washington, DC.

ॐ

Coming Soon!

GOD SISTERS

A NOVEL BY

KIMBERLY R. TAYLOR

Chapter One

At 12:45am, it had only been three hours since he'd left and in five hours, I'd be heading out the door to my corporate job that I loved to hate, both physically and emotionally tired. I wondered why I'd even allowed him to come over. And WHY, WHY, WHY did I sleep with him again? Just like the last time, I promised myself that this time would be the last time. "It wasn't like it was even good this time," I uttered into the air.

The television temporarily interrupted my thoughts with an infomercial for that ab buster thingy, the lazy sit up machine that does all the work for you. Right after that, there was another commercial for those 1-800 GURRRLS, blond nymphets, barely adults, who were waiting for a call...just waiting to fulfill a man's every fantasy.

Hmmph! What about my fantasy? What about commercials advertising for the Morris Chestnut substitute, extremely fine, dark chocolate skin, good job, sense of humor, educated, Christian, had money, single, not gay or on on the down low, not stuck on himself and good in all things in the bedroom. Most importantly, single like me, no kids or baby mama drama, few problems, no jail records and good credit. Now that would be a commercial worth producing. "*That* phone line would be on lock down with sisters from all over the country and other parts of the world, too." No one was listening but the TV, but still, it was worth saying out loud.

By all accounts, I wasn't supposed to be alone, especially since I had my mess together. One look at my resume, and a brother would know the good thing he was getting. I can cook, - from scratch too! Granted, not as good as my mother, but I can do a little something in the kitchen; those North Carolina recipes were burned in my memory.

As folk in the country say, I could keep house, too. It was important that a house was clean, but kept so people could enjoy living in it. Not so clean that no one felt welcome to sit on anything or sit longer than five minutes.

My academic credentials looked good too, B.S. from Temple University, Master's from Howard University and working on my PhD at American University. When I went away to school for undergrad, I didn't pay attention to the boys, just like the church mothers told me. They said, "Get your schooling, child," and I'd done just that. But it seemed that those who paid attention to the boys, got the husbands, kids, and the houses with the white picket fences. Those diplomas can only keep a girl warm at night if a match were thrown on them and a fire kindled! Anyway, corporate job? Check. Bonuses, benefits and stock options? Check, check and check. And if I do say so myself, I looked good too. I'm not a bony girl; didn't want to be. About size and weight, my cousin once remarked, "a dog doesn't want a bone with no meat." A girl like me from North Carolina could never turn down a good home cooked meal, especially my favorite comprised of fried pork chops, collard greens and macaroni and cheese, served with a diabetic inducing sugar filled glass of tea of course. At 5'7, I'm shapely, weighing in at about 185 which balanced out with those hereditary DD cups, everyone female in my family seemed to have. Definitely a credit to big girls everywhere.

So in my book it just didn't make sense. I had the goods; why didn't I have the man, who was all mine? This whole boyfriend -girlfriend thing didn't make sense. It was no longer simple. The days of boys meet girl; boy gets girl; and boy marries girl, and they lived happily ever after were certainly dead along with the last century. With the new millennium and the ratio of women to men 10 to 1, that story was boy meets girl; girl shares boy with girl, girl, girl and girl until somebody finds out. Then there's a fight - or an agreement to continue sharing. Then, sometimes it was boy meets girl and on occasion shares with boy. Then the sisters go to scrapping over the boy, while the boy meets another girl. And that could easily happen in church as well as on the streets. No place was safe from the African American male shortage. The shortage of eligible men seemed to lend more credence to brothers being serial monogamist, Monogamous meaning I' m seeing you, only when I'm with you. It was almost the most one could ask for these days.

Earlier that evening, the phone rang, displaying his number across my phone screen just as I turned my key in the door ready to retire after a long day at work. Unintentionally I counted the rings, not wanting to miss the call and knowing after the fourth ring it would go to voice mail. With a quick swipe of my finger, I answered.

"Bay," came from the other end. His mellowness both eased and stressed me out at the same time. Eve had her apple and he was mine, complete with the worm.

"Hey," was my simple response, attempting to match his relaxed tone.

"I' m about 20 minutes away from you, but my next job doesn't start until 9:00. We haven't seen each other in a while; can I come over for a little bit?"

Everything in me started screaming, "lie and say you're busy! Leave the house and say you're not home; tell him you've got company! But truth was I was soooo tired of coming home night after night with only the TV to keep me company. I always have a great time with my girlfriends, but lately, they weren't distraction enough. If I have to go to another movie, park or play with my girls, I'll lose my mind. So instead of just saying no, a wimpy, "you know where I live," came out.

"Aiight den, see you in about twenty minutes."

Now I had to pick up around the house; it wasn't really company-ready. Quickening my pace, I began shifting piles of bills and piles of clothes, neither of which I seemed to lack. It also seemed that no matter how much I picked them up, rearranged them and found special places for them, the piles were always there. Generally when I came in, my routine is to pull off my clothes while hot-footing it to the bathroom doing the pee-pee dance, and rummage through the day's mail. By the time I flush the toilet and leave the bathroom, I'm in my pajamas and a nice trail of my clothes sprinkle the hallway back to the living room, showing where I'd been. For the next few hours, my one true and constant companion usually keeps me company – my TV, but tonight real company was coming and I could use a little testosterone in my mix.

With a quick glance, I surveyed the room. It was presentable with two minutes to spare, which I used to make sure I had my look together.

While looking in the mirror, I brushed my hand across my honey colored skin; flawless and not so much as a blemish. High cheek bones, hazel eyes, my hair done every two weeks in a professional classic bob-cut, nothing too fancy. Because I religiously wrapped it at night, it needed very little attention. Just a little tousle and African Coconut oil sheen in the mornings and I was set. Fingers and toes perfectly manicured, clear polish only, home grown, no tips. I turned to check my back side and smiled at myself. Great clothes that complimented my figure. I was still conservative, to the heart, but moving to the city, helped me to experiment with bolder colors, cuts and styles of clothes I would not have dared tried in my home state. Today's look was a wonderful cream bolero pant suit, with a tangerine silk shell as an accent, and a natural, handmade African beaded necklace, earring and bracelet set. The multi colored earth tones well complimented the cream and tangerine ensemble. This outfit was my way of christening the wonderful spring day. The winter had been soo bleak and cooold and downright unforgiving some days, not to mention plain unbearable at night. So when the weatherman said temps in the low '70's I could hardly wait to get rid of my sweaters and other bulky clothes, at least for today.

I nodded my head in approval, but honestly, I don't know why I even made the effort, or cared how my place looked, and why I went through the drama of straightening things up, when in the end it didn't matter. Because he was married.

Here's how you can connect with the author:
Website: www.krtaylor.org
E-mail: kimtastically@gmail.com
Twitter: kimtastically
Facebook: Kimberly Taylor
Instagram: AuthorKRTaylor

Made in the USA
Middletown, DE
10 June 2016